10 Things
New Teachers
Need to
SUCCEED

SECOND EDITION

I dedicate this book with love to my only son, Timothy, who became my teacher over several years, teaching me more about who I am than I could ever have imagined.

10 Things New Teachers Need to SUCCEED

SECOND EDITION

Robin Fogarty

CORWIN PRESS
A SAGE Publications Company
Thousand Oaks, CA 91320

For information:

Corwin Press
A Sage Publications Company
2455 Teller Road
Thousand Oaks, California 91320
www.corwinpress.com

Sage Publications India Pvt. Ltd.
B 1/I 1 Mohan Cooperative Industrial Area
Mathura Road, New Delhi 110 044
India

Sage Publications Ltd.
1 Oliver's Yard
55 City Road
London EC1Y 1SP
United Kingdom

Sage Publications Asia-Pacific Pte. Ltd.
33 Pekin Street #02-01
Far East Square
Singapore 048763

Printed in the United States of America.

Library of Congress Cataloging-in-Publication Data

Fogarty, Robin.
Ten things new teachers need to succeed / Robin Fogarty. — 2nd ed.
    p. cm.
Includes bibliographical references and index.
ISBN-13: 978-1-4129-3892-1 (cloth)
ISBN-13: 978-1-4129-3893-8 (pbk.)
    1. First year teachers. 2. Teaching—Vocational guidance. I. Title.
LB2844.1.N4F64 2007
371.1—dc22   2007002107

This book is printed on acid-free paper.

08   09   10   11   10   9   8   7   6   5   4   3   2

Acquisitions Editor:	Hudson Perigo
Editorial Assistant:	Cassandra Harris
Production Editor:	Diane S. Foster
Copy Editor:	Carol Anne Peschke
Typesetter:	C&M Digitals (P) Ltd.
Proofreader:	Andrea Martin
Indexer:	Karen A. McKenzie
Cover Designers:	Monique Hahn and Scott Van Atta
Graphic Designer:	Lisa Miller

Contents

Preface

Having agreed to write a little book for new teachers, I tried to recall the things new teachers had said to me over the years. I sat down to list my ideas for the 10 things I thought teachers needed to survive and to thrive in the teaching profession. I wanted to see whether I could actually list just 10 things and what those 10 things might be.

I was joyful in the task and rendered my thoughts on paper as fast as I could type them. I knew I had hit the mother lode. I had discovered a way to expose the heart and soul of this time-honored gift called teaching. In fact, I realized that I had often said these things many times as I talked with teachers around the world about the art and science of teaching.

My wish for you—the reader, the new teacher, the mentor teacher, the math teacher, the music teacher, the favorite teacher, the remembered teacher, the substitute teacher, or the second career teacher—is that my words speak to you and your teaching, that they guide you and inspire you to continue with this very important work called teaching.

> "Come to the edge," he said.
>
> They said, "We are afraid."
>
> "Come to the edge," he said.
>
> They came.
>
> He pushed them . . . and they flew.
>
> —*Apollinaire*

A challenge from my constructivist grounding that I just cannot resist is to invite you to note the 10 things you would put on the list. Then, as you read, you'll have the satisfaction of seeing how well your thinking meshed with mine.

1.

2.

3.

4.

5.

6.

7.

8.

9.

10.

Enjoy!

—Robin Fogarty
Chicago, IL

Acknowledgments

I want to acknowledge two distinct and separate groups that are, in the end, inextricably entwined: mentees or protégés and mentors or mentor advocates.

Mentees and Protégés

The first group that warrants my gratitude consists of new teachers I have had the privilege to know, for their honest conversations, genuine frustrations, and willingness to grow.

Tiffany Fegley Krubert, formerly of Pritzker School, Chicago Public Schools, currently busy raising her children, Jack and Haley

Kathy Dopp, fifth-grade teacher, mentor and coach for the "Olympics of the Mind" championship team, Canajoharie School District, Canajoharie, New York

Molly Moynahan, author and teacher, formerly of Senn High School, Chicago Public Schools, currently teaching English at Evanston Township High School, Evanston, Illinois

Esme Raji Codell, formerly of the Chicago Public Schools, currently author, activist, and advocate for the teacher's voice

Mentors and Mentor Advocates

The second group that deserves mention is the new breed of mentors and coaches that I have had the honor to know, for their unrivaled expertise, constant dedication, and enormous contribution to their professional calling.

Arlene Fleischmann, Jeanne North, and Merry Mercer, Baltimore County Schools Mentor Program in Baltimore County, Maryland

Gene Kerns, former teacher and mentor for National Board Professional Certification, currently vice-president of training at Renaissance Learning

Mary Ellen Kotz, former teacher and mentor for National Board Professional Certification, currently director of the Delaware DOE Mentor Program

Diane Ray, director, Professional Association of Georgia Educators (PAGE) STAR Teacher Program, and assistant leader of Teacher Leader Development

Debra Zych, former director of Delaware DOE Lead Teachers and Mentors, currently assistant superintendent of New Castle County Voc/Tech High School in Wilmington, Delaware

The contributions of the following reviewers are gratefully acknowledged:

Jeanne Adele Kentel
Assistant Professor
Brock University
St. Catharines, Ontario, Canada

Tammy L. Lacey
Elementary School Principal
Loy Elementary School
Great Falls, Montana

Lori L. Grossman
Instructional Coordinator
Professional Development Services
Houston Independent School District
Houston, Texas

Mary Alice Barksdale
Associate Professor
Virginia Polytechnic Institute and State University
Blacksburg, Virginia

Rodger J. Beatty
Associate Dean, Faculty of Education
Brock University
St. Catharines, Ontario, Canada

About the Author

 **Robin Fogarty** received her doctorate in curriculum and human resource development from Loyola University of Chicago. A leading proponent of the thoughtful classroom, Fogarty has trained educators throughout the world in curriculum, instruction, and assessment strategies. She has taught at all levels, from kindergarten to college, served as an administrator, and consulted with state departments and ministries of education in the United States, Puerto Rico, Russia, Canada, Australia, New Zealand, Germany, Great Britain, Singapore, Korea, and the Netherlands. She has published articles in *Educational Leadership*, *Phi Delta Kappan*, and the *Journal of Staff Development*. She is the author or coauthor of numerous publications, including *Brain-Compatible Classrooms* (2001), *Literacy Matters* (2001), *How to Integrate the Curricula* (2002), *The Adult Learner* (2007), *A Look at Transfer* (2007), *Close the Achievement Gap* (2007), *Twelve Brain Principles That Make the Difference* (2007), *Nine Best Practices That Make the Difference* (2007), and *From Staff Room to Classroom: A Guide for Planning and Coaching Professional Development* (2006).

Introduction

I am a teacher. I've been a teacher for more than 30 years, knowing from the time I was 10 that teaching was what I was going to do. Like many new teachers who are reading this book, I love children; I gravitate to them and they to me. I love the act of creating, of inventing, of writing. Like so many teachers, I am a people person who likes to be in the midst of the action (an appropriate gift for those who choose to be in a room with 30 busy ones), and I am well schooled in the art and science of teaching.

My BA in early childhood and elementary education is from the State University of New York at Potsdam; my MA in instructional strategies is from National–Louis University in Evanston, Illinois; and my PhD in curriculum and instruction and human resource development is from Loyola University at Chicago.

I taught in the classroom for 17 years and in the staff room for 22 years. I had a very active personnel folder that tracked my placements in teaching from early childhood classrooms, to the primary grades, then fifth grade. I then moved into a team-teaching situation in a multiage classroom (8- to 12-year-olds). At one point in my career, I was a junior high substitute teacher for a year and finally worked my way into gifted education in elementary programs and in high school enrichment programs. I loved the creativity and the variety that my teaching career offered me, and I loved all of my assignments for the various challenges they presented. I am currently a staff development consultant, teaching teachers in professional development programs.

My vision of this little book is one of high aspirations. I see it sitting beside the great "little books" of my lifetime, such as Strunk and White's *Elements of Style,* Robert Pirsig's *Zen and the Art of Motorcycle Maintenance,* and Laurence Peter's *Peter's Quotations: Ideas for Our Time.* These are the texts that fit the spirit of my vision. I see my book becoming the well-worn desk copy, the quick reference, the on-hand authority for new and renewing teachers. I see tattered pages of yellowed paper, crimped corners, and underlinings of favorite passages revisited again and again. I see teachers sharing and comparing their originals with the new editions to check for any discrete changes or to see whether the new copy is really any different from the familiar old version treasured for so many years.

I hope this little book will become a cherished companion that is savored by seasoned staff and bestowed on new graduates as the quintessential gift. I see this little book as my gift to the profession— a giving back to the courageous ones who strive to teach. In my eyes, it is both a way of previewing the skill involved in the act of teaching and, perhaps more importantly, a way of renewing the spirit of those who teach.

As the book has evolved into the "new-teacher-must-have" category, two additional elements have evolved with the text. One is the visual element of film clips; the other is a professional development activity to complement the reading and discussions for each chapter.

The video clips are gleaned from the classic teacher films of the ages. Each film is slotted to accompany a chapter, used as a lead-in or accompaniment or even as a reflection piece. The 5- to 8-minute segments target the essence of the 10 topics. The films are listed in the Table of Contents. Discussion questions are listed in the chapter discussions.

In addition, a relevant professional development activity is included in each chapter to use as part of a monthly meeting with new teachers. It is aligned with the film clip to provide a viable and comprehensive session, complete with readings, discussions, and debriefing questions.

Though not written as a detailed how-to, *Ten Things New Teachers Need to Succeed* opens the conversation among educators ripe for dialogue about the intricacies of a complex profession. It is also perfect for a book study. Some might see this book as a checklist that profiles the critical areas of teaching expertise that make or break that new teacher.

The book's intended audience is aspiring teachers, preservice teachers who are just learning about teaching methods, new teachers preparing for their first teaching position, substitute teachers working their way into a first full-time position, or experts entering the profession as second career teachers. *Ten Things New Teachers Need to Succeed* is a glimpse into the world of the teacher.

HOW TO DO A BOOK STUDY

This is the perfect little book for a book study approach within the new teacher induction program or as part of the mentoring program within the district or the schools.

The following is a book study approach for the reader's consideration.

One District's Story

The principals and the staff development team selected a book, *Close the Achievement Gap: Simple Strategies That Work*, by Pete and Fogarty, for districtwide distribution to all staff. Then, each school in the district created book study teams that made sense to them. Some did grade-level teams, department teams, or core academic teams. Yet each team became a community of learners as they decided how they would study the book. Ideas ranged from discussion questions to role-plays, from strategy sessions to partner debriefings.

The defining piece involved two scheduled professional development sessions with the authors. One session in the fall and one session in the winter were held to bring the ideas in the book alive and to demonstrate the strategies for immediate application in K–12 classrooms. This model of professional development epitomized the best practices in professional development for the adult learner. The professional learning was sustained over a year. It was job embedded, collegial, and integrated with various elements of text, people-to-people interactions, and professional presentations. In addition, the professional learning was highly interactive and extremely practical.

The Perfect Book Study

Step 1: Establish instructional goals, select districtwide book

Step 2: Create communities of learners, building-level study teams

Step 3: Share book study ideas, select and schedule team approach

Step 4: Plan professional development presentation to bring the book alive

Step 5: Incorporate online professional development: New Explorations in Learning (when applicable)

Step 1: Instructional Goals: Districtwide Book

- Analyze district data.
- Determine instructional goals.
- Align to school improvement plan.

Step 2: Community of Learners, Building-Level Study Teams

- Grade-level teams
- Department teams
- Core academic teams
- One wing of building
- Vertical teams (across grade levels)
- Self or preselected teams

Step 3: Book Study Ideas

- Chapter by chapter: Teams present information
- Literature circles: Team develops and discusses questions
- Key concepts: Team role-plays ideas
- Applications of ideas: Team directs strategies to try
- Independent reading: Team debriefs in pairs
- Written summaries: Team creates graphic organizers

Step 4: Professional Development Presentation to Bring the Book Alive

- External consultant provides professional development presentations.
- Building teams provide professional development presentations.
- Building teams are sent to partner building to share ideas.

Step 5: Online Professional Development

- Incorporate online professional development programs as an option to support the books.
- Web site: www.newexplorationsinlearning.com.

A Book Study Activity to Try: Cooperative Learning Tear and Share

Instructions (teams of four):

1. Everyone reads entire piece on "The Perfect Book Study."

2. Everyone responds to all four questions in the following form.

3. Teams count off by fours; tear paper into four sections and pass appropriate numbered section to that numbered person or group.

4. Team members preview all four responses for their number and give an oral summary.

5. Open discussion follows after all have shared.

1. Describe a professional development book study. A book study is like _____ (concrete object) because both _____ _____ (comparison).	2. Rank the preferred study team organization. ___ Grade or department team ___ Wing of building ___ Vertical team (across grade levels) ___ Cross-departmental team
3. Explain how a professional development session and book study might go together.	4. List three possible professional books or topics for a possible book study.

SOURCE: www.robinfogarty.com.

Recommended Nutshell Books
- *How to Differentiate*
- *Close the Achievement Gap*
- *Data! Dialogue! Decision!*
- *Nine Best Practices*

The Monthly Meeting

Although the book study option is spelled out in five simple steps, others use this book a bit differently. Some use a chapter a month to kick off meetings with new teachers. They assign a particular chapter for prereading. Then they start the meeting with the video clip or DVD chapter recommended from noteworthy films about teaching. A debriefing follows, highlighting key points from the designated chapter and the film. In turn, the professional development activity helps to anchor the learning of the day. It also provides a practical idea for new teachers to take directly back to their classrooms to use with their students. This format is a high-energy way to get new teachers talking about the key elements of the teaching profession.

1

A Knowing Colleague as Counsel

About the Policies, Practices, and Politics

Without a doubt, the number one priority for the new teacher is to have a friend in the school, on the premises, visible, available, and accessible, a knowing colleague on staff who is there for the new kid on the block. After many conversations with first- and second-year teachers (some who stayed in the profession and others who chose to leave within the first few years), I've noticed teachers invariably talk about the need for someone they can count on, someone they can go to when they have questions and when they need help, someone who is there when they need a mentor and even when they don't.

Although many districts establish formal new teacher induction programs that include an assigned mentor for each new teacher, not all schools have the resources to do this. Therefore, with two and a half million new teachers expected to enter the field over the next 10 years and with the growing exodus of seasoned staff into retirement, it seems wise for new teachers to assume responsibility for finding the person they need: a friend, a coach, a mentor.

PROACTIVELY SEEK A MENTOR

New teachers can't wait for someone to be assigned as mentor or for a friend to emerge from the ranks. Even when they are assigned a formal mentor, they may need to proactively seek out a caring colleague. They must find someone who exhibits qualities they admire: a solid knowledge base, a sense of humor, or a manner of working with the students. It must be someone who resonates with them and their core values. They must find someone who is right for them and who is available when they need help.

They must find someone familiar with district policies, who understands how the district runs the testing program and knows what to do with the mountain of memos that come from the central office. They need to find someone who knows how to work within the current practices regarding required textbooks and understands the accepted role of academic freedom in the district.

New teachers must find someone familiar with building practices who knows how to get around the school and the grounds. New teachers must find someone who understands the rules and regulations and accepted practices regarding lunchtime, recess, study hall, absences, discipline, report cards, parent calls, Internet use, and other things that occur regularly in the day of the classroom teacher.

The novice needs to find someone who knows the politics of the school faculty. Who knows what and whom? Who gets things done, and who blocks things from getting done? Who are the informal leaders, and how much power do they have? Who is most likely to welcome the role of coach or mentor? Whom do they want as their friend and knowing colleague? The new teacher needs the friendship of a kindred spirit and the wisdom of a seasoned veteran. The new teacher needs this sage to survive and thrive.

> The new teacher needs the friendship of a kindred spirit and the wisdom of a seasoned veteran.

Film Clip: *Finding Forrester*

Focus: Mentoring

Find the sections in which Forrester is coaching the boy about how to write. Forrester says things like, "Hit those keys. Write like you know what you're saying. Just write words, any words, the same words, until a thought comes to you. Write the first draft from your heart, write the second with your head."

Questions

How does Forrester, a renowned author and mentor in the film, demonstrate the power of one-on-one mentoring? Cite several examples from the film clip in which the mentor instructs, encourages, empowers, and inspires.

Suggested Activity: A Mediated Journal Entry

(Mentor reads aloud the prompts as the mentees respond in writing.)

1. Name someone who is a mentor (historical figure, fictional character, life acquaintance).

2. List two qualities of this mentor.

3. Describe someone who is not a mentor.

4. Explain how the two are different.

5. Write a concluding statement.

6. Title your piece.

7. Share it with a colleague.

2

A Place Called "My Room" for Students to Grow, to Groom, and to Zoom

In a place called school is the place called "my room." This room, the classroom, is sacred territory to teachers. It is their proclaimed domain, and the room projects the beliefs, values, and personality of the teacher. Teachers know this to be true: The classroom belongs to the teacher and to his or her kids! It is an extension of who that teacher is and how he or she wants to project formal learning to the students.

> The classroom belongs to the teacher and to his or her kids!

It speaks of the teacher's education and training, philosophies, priorities, and passions. It speaks volumes to the students they teach and the parents they meet.

CREATE A LEARNING ENVIRONMENT THAT FOSTERS GROWTH AND PRIDE

If the room presents a rich environment, genuine student involvement results. It demonstrates that richness in black and white—and greens and reds and yellows—in maps and charts and potted plants, in bulletin boards, student supplies, science equipment, computer gear, and student desks and chairs. If the room speaks of student papers, works of art, time for thinking deeply, pondering and puzzling, then this room speaks of the teacher's expectations for the students who call this place "my room."

If the room evokes a rigorous learning environment where effort is applauded, a challenging culture where risk is expected, and a protected zone of emotional safety where every student feels respected and honored and included, then surely it is a room that invites learners to grow emotionally as well as intellectually.

If the room inspires peak performances for every learner to become all he or she is capable of becoming, if it inspires habits of mind for precision in work, persistence in effort, and perfection in performance, then surely this is the place for students to excel, each in his or her own way.

The classroom is the place where students can grow and groom and zoom. The words "my room" evoke a feeling of pride in the teacher and the students, who know it well from the inside out. Remember, it is in this room that students develop intellectually. It is the place where they "grow and groom" physically, and it is the place where they "zoom" as individuals in peak performance for every encounter. Teachers understand that the term "my room" doesn't really mean their room but, rather, the students' room. It is the place where it all happens that year, and it is up to the teacher to design with forethought and care for the eventful occasions sure to occur.

Film Clip: *Pay It Forward*

Focus: Learning Environment

Find the sections in this film in which the teacher sets expectations for the love of language, learning of new words, and a print-rich environment in which to learn. He says things like this:

"Atrophy? If you don't know a word . . . you will look it up in these dictionaries that you will take with you wherever you go. You're going to learn to love words in this classroom."

Questions

How does the teacher create a learning environment? Cite several instances from the film clip that exemplify a rich and robust learning environment, a classroom in which students have the resources and the responsibility to use them.

Suggested Activity: Bulletin Boards

Develop a striking bulletin board that supports a current unit of study. Include key information for students to peruse. Discuss the fact that we learn through both focused and peripheral attention, according to the brain principles (Caine, Caine, McClintic, & Klimek, 2004), and that bulletin boards that support learning are valuable peripheral learning tools. Kids will notice them explicitly or implicitly, but either way, they will absorb the information.

3

A Method for Managing 1,500 Decisions on Your Seat and on Your Feet

It has been said that a classroom teacher makes 1,500 decisions in a day. Some of those decisions are on-your-seat decisions that occur in the quiet moments of planning and plotting the course of action—or the reaction to the teaching and learning experiences. Other decisions are on-your-feet decisions that occur in the heat of action, when the dust has not yet settled and a teacher's mind is on a number of things at once. To stay sane, the teacher needs a method for managing this multitude of decisions. In fact, the teacher needs many methods for doing things that match with the myriad things that need doing.

On-your-seat decisions include schedules, charts, and calendars, units of study, lesson plans, and weekly quizzes. Teachers need a one-page schedule that lists their day-to-day responsibilities. They need a calendar of events that plots weekly and monthly happenings. Teachers need posters and bulletin boards that bring the notes and the news into their rooms. They need a seating chart—in pencil, because it may change frequently. Teachers need a planning book to document in writing the upcoming curriculum units and their detailed daily lesson plans. They need a grade book to record the grades that make up the final grade, and they need a notebook to note last-minute changes that make each day different than originally planned.

LET COMMON SENSE RULE
THE MOMENT OF DECISION

In the category of on-your-feet decisions are many things that disrupt the day. Throughout the day, a teacher's radar is up for the waves of data he or she must detect. Teachers must decide who is bored, challenged, or frustrated and what plans of action to use to move each student forward. Teachers must decide how much or how little to review from the previous day's lesson and how hard or how easy to make Friday's pop quiz. Teachers must decide, in the midst of the action, whom to give more challenge in reading or math and whom to give more in-depth review. Teachers must decide, on the spot, whose story is reliable and who is liable. They must intervene and convene on a moment's notice. Teachers must decide any number of things in the course of a day, and to do this with wisdom and wit is no easy task. The best bet is to observe and assess situations as well as one can and let common sense rule the moment of decision. Later reflection usually can rectify a regrettable decision. Although this constant flow of activity demands the absolute and undivided attention of the teachers, decision making becomes easier, or at least more familiar, with time. The ebb and flow of the classroom settles into an established set of routines and

> Teachers must decide any number of things in the course of a day, and to do this with wisdom and wit is no easy task.

> After much practice, patience, and persistence, at some point along the way the new teacher becomes able to fly on autopilot.

regimes. Eventually, after much practice, patience, and persistence, at some point along the way the new teacher becomes able to fly on autopilot.

Film Clip: *Teachers*

Focus: Rules, Regs, and Routines

Find the scene in which the traditional teacher is sitting in the back of the room. The kids come in, find the "ditto of the day" that is waiting on the stack in a predetermined spot, do the ditto, and place it back on another stack as they leave the classroom. Throughout the scene, the teacher sits at his desk, hidden behind an open newspaper. Ironically, in the final moment of the scene, the teacher is shown flopped over, presumably unnoticed yet quite obviously dead.

Questions

Begin by discussing the humor of the scene. Then proceed with a more weighty discussion about how teachers create routines for workflow, for moving about and in and out of the classroom, for typical classroom activities that create a workable ebb and flow. What tricks of the trade have new teachers learned for organizing and managing their classroom?

Suggested Activity: That's a Good Idea

"That's a Good Idea" is a social skill exercise that focuses on attentive listening. In pairs, one person tells and the other affirms by saying, "That's a good idea because. . . ."

For the new teacher session, have two colleagues use the "That's a Good Idea" format for a structured dialogue about the two kinds of decisions the teacher makes day in and day out. Do one round with the focus on "On-my-seat decision I made . . ." and the response, "That's a good idea because. . . ." Then do a second round with the lead in, "On-my-feet decision I made . . ." and the same response, "That's a good idea because. . . ." Debrief on how it feels to be affirmed for decisions you have made.

4

A Discipline Plan That Works on Paper and on Students

A sometimes troublesome task for the new teacher is student discipline. From the moment they leave for school until long after the final bell sounds, students are interacting passively, assertively, or aggressively. Dealing with discipline decisions can be the most time-consuming part of the job in the early days, weeks, and months of teaching.

Discipline problems range from the daily squabbles of younger students (fighting on the playground over who owns the ball and who goes first), to the bothersome pranks of rambunctious teens (creating graffiti on the buildings or teasing one another), to chronic tardiness, absenteeism, and unacceptable hallway behavior, to escalating violence on the bus, in the lunchroom, or in the schoolyard.

There is no way to bypass this part of teaching, yet there are ways to lighten the load of disciplinary concerns for the new teacher. The first line of defense is to establish a written discipline plan that is clearly posted for all to see and heed. The written plan delineates the rules of the classroom and, ideally, the consequences for breaking the rules. As the teacher developing the discipline plan, keep in mind that less is more. Keep the number of rules manageable by limiting them to high-priority concerns: safety of the students, fairness for all, and work ethics that spell success.

This classroom discipline plan often is created with student input. Some think it is better for students to have a say so they feel ownership of the plan and therefore are more likely to respect and adhere to the agreements made. Others develop the plan before the first day of school and have the rules boldly displayed for the first rigorous discussion about expected student behavior and delineated consequences for misbehavior. Whatever the method of development, the plan needs to align with district and school policies, and it must be shared explicitly with the students and parents.

BE CONSISTENT, BE FLEXIBLE

The second line of defense in handling student discipline is not as neat and tidy as the first. This second concern is the reaction of the teacher when the infraction occurs or immediately after a problem surfaces. The advice often given by discipline gurus is to be *consistent* and, at the same time, to be *flexible*. At first glance, this message seems contradictory. How can a teacher be consistent and flexible at the same time?

Upon further examination this message does contain the seeds of wisdom in dealing with the human factor. The teacher must be consistent in interpreting the rules and consequences. At the same time, the teacher needs to know when to ask for help from the many who are there to serve the students: a social worker for a constantly tired, hungry student; the principal for the student who will not obey posted rules or whose parents won't respond to requests or inquiries; security personnel for a student in possession of a weapon.

> Teachers must make ad hoc decisions quickly, firmly, and confidently, for the kids are watching.

At the same time, the teacher also needs to be flexible in understanding and allowing for extenuating circumstances and individual factors. Use your best judgment and manage the incident with the least amount of distraction from the lesson and the least amount of embarrassing focus on the violator. Don't feed into his or her conscious or subconscious need for attention. Use common sense and trust your plan. Students want to know what the parameters are, and they respect the rules of the classroom if they are enforced consistently.

Teachers must make ad hoc decisions quickly, firmly, and confidently, for the kids are watching. These kids are aware, and they can't be fooled easily. Teachers must show that they are in charge by the way they look, feel, and act. And in the first days of school, the first impressions of order and flow, of management and control, become the lasting impressions of students caught in these interactions and reactions.

Film Clip: *To Sir, With Love*

Focus: Expectations

Find the clip of the classroom scene in which the inner-city schoolteacher lays down the rules of law and the rules of etiquette for this unconventional group of inner-city, senior high school ruffians. Note the lofty aspirations he has for proper behavior and his high expectations of formality and propriety for his interesting but insolent students.

Questions

Discuss the paradox of kids who act out and demonstrate rude and rough behaviors yet respond appropriately to well-defined structure, established routines, and clear and decisive parameters. Also explore the role of classroom rules and explicit consequences.

Suggested Activity: Reader's Theater and the Morph Grid

Reader's Theater: In pairs, students A and B take turns reading every other line.

Selection: "Sarah Cynthia Silvia Stout Who Would Not Take the Garbage Out," Shel Silverstein poem from *Where the Sidewalk Ends*.

Morphological Grid of Options: Use the morph grid to make explicit the possible players involved when student behavior warrants disciplinary action: the teacher, the student, the principal, the parent. In this poem, the student is at home, but it illustrates in an engaging way the many options one has, and it addresses the concept of appropriateness of a consequence.

Then, in table teams, roll the dice four times, once for each of the four roles. Determine and discuss the appropriateness of the various remedies that emerge for managing the insolent child who would not take the garbage out. New teachers and mentors using this activity will need to use their imaginations a little bit because the misbehavior does not actually occur in school. Yet the richness of these discussions sets the stage for future talks about real situations in the classroom. As a bonus, mentors get a chance to introduce new teachers to Silverstein's books.

Debrief about appropriate and inappropriate reactions and the complexities of managing student behavior. Use this memorable discussion activity as a pivot point for other conversations.

Teacher Action	Student Response	Parent Involvement	Principal Notification
1. Take aside	Explain behavior	Ground for a week	Expel from school
2. Ignore	Write about why	Assign another chore	Suspend for 1 day
3. Proximity	Apologize	Put in time out	Stay out of it
4. Reprimand	Promise to change	Send to room	Talk to student
5. Dismiss	Withdraw	Suspend allowance	Call counselor

5

A Standard Understanding of the Almighty Standards

A standard understanding of the standards is definitely the standard for teachers in contemporary schools. Standards delineate the student achievement goals of the curriculum. Standards of learning clarify and quantify the most important content in the various subject matter areas. At the same time, standards target lifelong skills and processes (thinking, organizing, socializing, and technology) that are necessary for a solid education to occur. Yet there is an important distinction to make.

> Standards are not the curriculum. They are the goals of the curriculum.

Standards are not the curriculum. They are the goals of the curriculum. Teachers don't teach the standards, they teach the curriculum, and in the process they help students achieve the standards. For example, if the standard states, "All students are able to communicate effectively in written and oral communication," the teaching of the communication skills may be accomplished through work with their interpretation of *The Red Badge of Courage*. Or the skills may be addressed through a science curriculum in which students prepare a written and oral presentation about a genetic disease. In both scenarios, the standard of effective communication is clustered with standards in other areas. The standard of learning certainly is one of the overriding goals, but in one case the curriculum centers around the study of a novel, and in the other situation the curriculum focuses on the study of a biology unit.

CLUSTER STANDARDS
INTO CURRICULUM CONTENT

The real concern for teachers is their knowledge and understanding of the standards: knowing the accepted and established content priorities and understanding how the process standards, such as higher-order thinking and cooperative skills, weave into the fabric of the content. The real work of teachers is in aligning the standards to the curriculum they are required to teach and in clustering the standards with that curriculum content.

Only through intricate texturing of the standards into complex student performances can teachers address the overwhelming number of standards properly. If teachers try to lay the standards end to end and approach them in a sequential manner, they will never reach the end of the line; there are simply too many standards for that direct approach to work effectively and efficiently.

Requiring middle school students to take on the role of newspaper publishers for a history unit about their hometown is the kind of complex task that illustrates how teachers layer and texture a cluster of standards. Within the task of creating a mock newspaper that depicts an era of history in the town, content standards involving historical data become the history content focus. Process standards of research skills, language usage, and written and oral communication skills are addressed as students interview and research and gather the facts of the times. The technology skills of word processing and graphic arts are integrated as students design and prepare the paper for publication.

In addition, the skills of teamwork and compromise and reaching agreements are interwoven in arriving at the final product.

Significant habits of mind, such as pride in one's work and persistence at a task, are bonus standards that are part of the robust performance requirements. This is how teachers design curriculum to meet student learning standards, not by addressing the standard as the content. Complex performance tasks are compelling to students, whereas working on a discrete standard by itself reduces the teaching and learning scenario to what is commonly known as a skill-and-drill curriculum. It's easy to discern which method students respond to and deserve. And it's easy to tell which method teachers prefer if they are to meet the many standards embedded in their various curricula.

Film Clip: *Best of Saturday Night Live: Seinfeld* (History Lesson Episode)

Focus: Standards of Excellence Through Student Learning Standards (Content and Process)

Use the entire skit, which is about 8 minutes. Discuss the idea of rigor through higher-order thinking and questioning strategies. Have the new teachers track the number of questions Seinfeld asks in the history class. Then debrief about the effectiveness of the questioning.

Questions

Discuss the role of standards in a rigorous and rich curriculum. Were they higher-order thinking questions? How might they foster inquiry learning?

Activity: Journaling With Writing Prompts

The reflective journal is one of the most powerful tools to use when mentoring new teachers. Occasionally assigning selected topics for timed writing entries adds an interesting dimension of rigor. Try one of the following topics for this exercise. Then suggest that teachers try some of these topics with their students just to see how they respond to a timed exercise, such as a 1-minute challenge, and to examine the quality of their writing.

General Topics

> I shoulda, coulda, woulda . . .
>
> I remember . . .
>
> I regret . . .
>
> I cherish . . .
>
> I laughed . . .
>
> I wish . . .

Topics About Writing

> I never thought I could write like this
>
> It's not hard to write: It's my story
>
> Writing on cue: It's easy!
>
> Oh, how I wish I could write like that

Topics About Science

> Experimenting in science is . . .
>
> My favorite area of science is . . .

Topics in Social Studies

> The country I most want to visit is . . .
>
> The election
>
> Foreign language
>
> I want to learn _____ because _____
>
> A culture that fascinates me is _____

6

A Known Knowledge Base of Core Curriculum Content

A first-year teacher confessed her worst nightmare in a letter about her concerns as a new professional. She said, plainly and painfully, "I have the standards and I have the curriculum materials, but I really don't know what I am supposed to teach. I know I can't do all of this, but I don't really know what is most important. I'm not sure how other teachers sort it all out and make sense of the curriculum."

This may seem a bit naïve to seasoned staff members, but if they think about a time they taught a new course or changed grade levels, they have a sense of what new teachers face as they try to make sense of the curriculum.

"What are the real priorities?" is the question that haunts novices. How do they attack the avalanche of material before them? How do they begin to sort it out and set curricular priorities? How do seasoned staff make curricular decisions about what elements of the curriculum get the most weight? In essence, what are the essential standards and what are the supplemental standards?

> **If all of the standards were taught, schooling would move from a K–12 structure to a K–22 structure.**

The instinct of this novice is right on the mark. Even though the standards are delineated and the curriculum goals seem quite straightforward, the truth is that there are far too many content standards to actually teach each of the standards with equal weight. In fact, it has been said that if all of the standards were taught, schooling would move from a K–12 structure to a K–22 structure.

MAP THE COURSE,
THEN TALK WITH AN EXPERT

The best way for new teachers to tackle the needed knowledge base and the core content is to review the curriculum guides, texts, and supplemental materials for the grade level or department. Teachers then need to identify and gather these resources as soon as possible, even before the term begins. Once the resources are in hand, new teachers need to survey the guides, skim all the documents, and get a sense of the curriculum landscape. Then they need to make some preliminary notes, marking the units, topics, and concepts that make up the core content of the course or subject, which is the knowledge base that is essential to learning. At the same time, the teachers need to look over the standards again and think about how they integrate with the emerging curriculum scheme.

Armed with these notes of their first impression of the curricular priorities, new teachers must arrange to sit down with their mentor or a willing and knowledgeable colleague and discuss their ideas. Ideally, curriculum mapping has been a part of the standard planning, and this curriculum map is available. If that is the case, the new teacher needs to compare his or her thoughts with the existing curriculum map and plan.

If no curriculum mapping has occurred, the new teacher must have a conversation with a mentor or colleague to compare thoughts and talk about priorities of the grade level or department, the length of time for various learning experiences, the depth of study anticipated, and the sequence and timing devoted to the core pieces. Then, new teachers can devise a semester or annual schedule that synthesizes the big picture. In essence, together they create a curriculum map for the term to use as a road map for instructional planning.

During the discussion, the new teachers ask the experienced teachers questions about what and why and how. New teachers elicit as much information as possible about how decisions are made. They try to gain insight into why things are sorted out in certain ways and talk about best- and worst-case scenarios. They ask questions such as, "What happens if . . . ?" "How might I . . . ?" "Why do you . . . ?" and "What do you do when . . . ?" in anticipation of plausible situations.

This kind of core curriculum model presents a two-pronged process: developing an individual curriculum map and sharing and comparing the initial ideas with another teacher. In this way, new teachers can dig into the curriculum on their own to discern the key concepts. At the same time, they can share and compare their results with a knowing colleague. In addition, by beginning the conversation early in the term, they open the door to continued dialogue as the curriculum unfolds. Eventually, this leads to confidence in a known (identified, agreed to, and generally accepted) knowledge base and a better understanding of the core curriculum content.

Film Clip: *Master and Commander*

Focus: Lifelong Learning

Find the scene in which some of the crew set out on the Galápagos Islands to explore, investigate, and research the various species of insects and animals they find. In the scene the young boy observes, sketches, and writes each entry intently and in great detail. It is a wonderful scene to illustrate the multiple intelligences approach to curriculum and learning. It is inspirational in its message about how to get kids intensely involved in learning as they develop lifelong skills of precision, accuracy, and pride in their work.

Questions

How do teachers make critical decisions about an overloaded, overextended, and never-ending curriculum and distill the core knowledge base for each subject area? One response to this question provides fertile ground for discussion. The core curriculum should address the skills, concepts, and attitudes that students will need as they enter the world of work.

Activity: Curriculum Mapping

New teachers develop a list by month of what they think is most important from their survey of the learning standards, texts, and other supplementary materials. To assist them in making this list, several thoughts might guide their decision making in terms of what kids need to know and be able to do. Enduring learnings are the kinds of things in the curriculum that students will need for life: problem solving, thinking, conceptual understandings about conflict, cultures, change, symmetry, structures, and design. As new teachers look over their curriculum, this becomes their take on the core curriculum of essential or enduring learnings.

In the meantime, seasoned teachers and mentors can begin this discussion with new teachers by using a diary of their curriculum, by mapping what they actually teach in each subject area during various months of the school year. Using their diary maps, they can debrief with the new teachers as they compare their diary maps to what the new teachers have targeted from their investigation of the various materials available. It is a fruitful activity to begin the conversation about what to teach and why.

7

A Fail-Safe Lesson Design for Teachers to Teach and Learners to Learn

Skillful teaching is inextricably linked to lesson design. It is the hallmark of excellent teachers. As architects of the intellect, good teachers know just how to lay out the plans for fail-safe lessons. They truly understand the delicacy of the equation inherent in the teaching and learning process. They know how to include the essential elements with expert input, how to use a wide variety of resources, how to structure brain-friendly learning experiences, how to include students with special needs, how to give clear and concise instructions, and how to build accountability for student achievement. These intellectual architects know their craft well.

> As architects of the intellect, good teachers know just how to lay out the plans for fail-safe lessons.

In the blueprints they work with, they tease the learner with an inviting sketch that lures the students to the scene (anticipatory set). These architects get the interest of their patrons (the students, in this case) and hook them into the learning in multiple ways. They may use teacher talk and well-worn stories, invite a surprise guest to appear before the class, show a specially selected video clip, embark on an excursion around the school grounds, or stage a role-play to occur unexpectedly before an unknowing audience. Whatever they do, they do it deliberately, dramatically, and with intent. Their purpose is to engage the minds of these young people and to capture their interest.

These skillful architects then reveal the basic foundational pieces, giving students the core information and data they need to proceed (input). In this essential phase of the teaching and learning process, these architects design with great care. They share their understanding of their craft with simplicity and grace. They have studied their content so well that they know instinctively what is too much, what is not enough, and what is just the right amount of input for the learners. They use every resource they have to construct a solid and sound base. They use textbook knowledge, graphs and charts, posters, expert testimony, analogies, and metaphorical references. They use the specialized cognitive tools of the trade.

Next, these architects provide an exquisite model of the work with every detail in place (modeling). They unveil a three-dimensional model in all its glory, hoping to instruct, invite, and inspire future genius in these waiting protégés. They narrate a walking tour of the model, exposing its staid traditions, fundamental ornaments, and uniquely mounted features. The model is the quintessential specimen to revel in. It is the model to aspire to.

TEACH THEM, THEN COACH THEM

These knowing mentors then proceed with the design that brings the learner into the learning with intensely involving experiences. Students are divided into small, cooperative groups to encourage them to converse with each other in collaborative endeavors. Teachers make a number of critical decisions in forming the cooperative teams. They must decide on the composition or makeup of the groups, the size of the groups (two to four), the students' roles and responsibilities (material manager, recorder, reporter, encourager), the performance task, and how students are held accountable for learning. In these groups, students are expected to take responsibility as individuals and as a team, to solve problems and reach agreements, to produce, and to be individually accountable for the assignment. Giving step-by-step instructions, these architects scaffold the learning for the willing apprentices (guided practice) as they undertake the tasks of the group. Each phase is carefully laid out and scrutinized by the master for accuracy and likeness to the reigning model. In addition, the process is carefully observed for later feedback for the teams.

Offering expert guidance and on-site coaching along the way (monitoring and feedback), the masters advise and mentor these earnest young minds. Students are queried about their work and groups are assisted as needed. At this point the role of the master is to guide and facilitate the work with specific feedback, coaching, and continual encouragement. The architect notices the subtleties of each design and leads the group to define, redefine, and refine the work they do. The process is as important as the product, for it is the process that takes them along the journey to the next assignment.

Soon, the apprentices seem ready. They have demonstrated their abilities in the basics, and they are encouraged to use those developing skills to create a design of their own (independent practice). The assignment might be an in-class project that extends over time or some daily work, on their own, that shows evidence of their learning, or it may be a homework assignment that demonstrates their individual understanding of the concepts and skills. The goal at this point in the lesson design is for the master architect to determine how capable these apprentices really are. It is in this fail-safe lesson design that the architects of the intellect demonstrate their art and their skill. It is in this fail-safe lesson design that these architects share their gifts with eager new teachers.

Film Clip: *Dead Poets Society*

Focus: Teach Them and Coach Them

Find the scene in which Robin Williams introduces a poetry unit and tells the students to tear the pages from the text. Follow this humorous and poignant scene until he asks them, "What will your verse be?"

Questions

What are the elements of a good lesson design, and how and why are these elements vital to effective instruction?

Activity: Four-Fold Concept Lesson

The Four-Fold Activity is a strategy to build vocabulary and develop concepts. It can be used with an individual student, student pairs, or a small group of students. The paper, regular copy paper or large poster paper, depending on the number of students, is folded into four sections, as shown in Figure 7.1. When the paper is folded, the corners where the folds meet are turned down to create a triangle; when it is opened there will be a diamond shape in the center of the paper for the target word. Each of the four sections is labeled from top left to bottom right: LIST, RANK, COMPARE, ILLUSTRATE. Then each section is addressed as the students unpack the language of the target word.

In the example the target word is from language arts. It is the word *plot*, the plot of a story. Students follow these four steps:

Figure 7.1   Four-Fold Concept Development

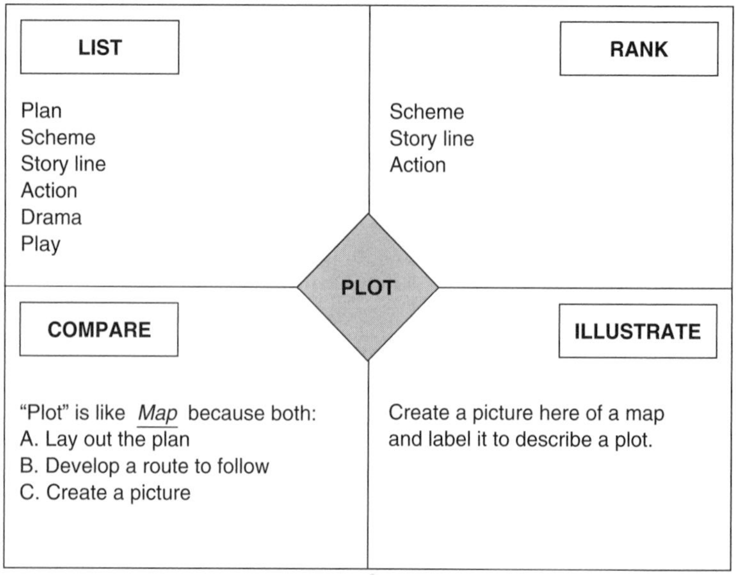

1. LIST: Brainstorm 15–20 synonyms.

2. RANK: Prioritize the best three words to clarify the word *plot*.

3. COMPARE: Students use the following to create an analogy: "Target Word" is like (Concrete/tangible word) because both:

   A.

   B.

   C.

4. ILLUSTRATE: Draw a visual metaphor of the analogy; make a poster.

Once the four steps are completed, students can share the information. The process helps develop vocabulary and concepts. It covers all the elements of engaged learning through an inviting lesson design. This lesson can be used with target words from any subject area. Possible words to use that are key concepts in the various disciplines might include the following:

Math: *distributive, associative, infinity, equal, algebra*

Language arts: *comprehension, literature, fiction, nonfiction*

Science: *energy, motion, environment, chemistry, physics*

Social sciences: *Bill of Rights, Civil War, citizenship, election*

Health and physical education: *wellness, sportsmanship, genes, muscles, nutrition*

Arts: *media, medium, sculpture, comedy, tragedy, opera*

To use the Four-Fold Concept Development with new teachers or staff groups, select words that are pertinent to them, and/or fit the district focus of: differentiation, formative assessments, professional learning communities, or collaborations.

8

A Repertoire of Teaching Strategies

Different Strokes for Different Folks

A repertoire of teaching strategies means exactly that: a growing list of instructional methods, options that tap into the many ways students know and understand. However it's done, a repertoire means more than one. The skillful teacher is aware of the differences in the students she or he teaches. Just think of the variety one finds in physical development. There are tall students and short students; students with long hair and students with short hair; students who are full-bodied and those who are slight and slender; students who are left-handed, right-handed, and even ambidextrous; there are students who are loud in their ways and those who try not to be noticed; there are students who are sleepy and those who are hungry.

Looking beyond these obvious and observable differences between the students in a class, imagine the not-so-obvious and not-so-observable differences in the cognitive functioning of these same students. There are students who write easily and well and those who dread written assignments; there are those who read fluently and with insight and others who

> However it's done, a repertoire means more than one.

have no clue; there are artistic types and others who are not able to visualize their thoughts; there are problem solvers and logical thinkers and others who would rather not have to deduce anything; there are youngsters who ride the waves of music and those who have little or no connection to popular melodies. There are students who are athletically fit and excel at many sports, and there are others who are always the last ones picked. There are students who lead, and there are those who follow; there are youngsters who revel in self-reflection and know themselves to perfection, and there are others who wonder aloud, "Who am I? Where am I going?" Students are different, period. Learners are different, and that means they may need different approaches to their learning.

TAP INTO THE TALENTS OF EACH LEARNER

Different strokes for different folks means a number of things to the skillful teacher. It means tapping Howard Gardner's theory and incorporating a multiple intelligences approach to the teaching and learning process. It means using verbal, visual, bodily, musical, mathematical, interpersonal, and intrapersonal experiences, the perspective of naturalists who understand the flora and fauna of the natural environment, and the existential intelligence used to ponder the complexities of the world.

Different strokes for different folks means differentiating instruction in multiple ways: Teachers can change the actual content, the learning environment, the instructional process, or the requirements for the product. In so doing, teachers attempt to meet the spectrum of talents and gifts of the students they teach. Changing the content may mean offering a selection of novels to read that focus on a common theme, such as friendship. Students choose the novel of interest or the reading level that is most comfortable. Changing the learning environment means using the resource center for the students who need quiet or allowing others to work with headphones on if they respond to music. Changing the process means letting some work in pairs for collaborative synergy and asking others to work as a team of four to accomplish individual tasks. Changing the product means encouraging students to use many ways of expressing what they know and are able to do as they present their information. They may use puppets, role-plays, a newscast, a radio talk show, written reports, or discussion groups.

Different strokes for different folks means problem-based learning, case studies, thematic instruction, projects, and service learning. It means performance learning, apprenticeships, internships, walkabouts, and excursions in the field or virtual trips online. Differentiated instruction means distance learning, classroom learning, brain-based learning, Web-based learning, and real-life learning. Differentiated learning means the teacher changes something to meet the needs, and sometimes the wants, of the learners.

Film Clip: *Akeelah and the Bee*

Focus: Cooperative Learning, Multiple Intelligences, and Higher-Order Thinking

Find the scene in the movie in which Akeelah uses a distinctive method (the rhythm of jumping rope) to cue her spelling of the words.

Questions

How does this scene in the spelling bee illustrate the need for differentiated instruction? Identify some of the methods and modalities and discuss how they are played out in the classroom. Then have them read and review the responses to the questions in the chapter.

Activity: Frequently Asked Questions for In-Depth Understanding

Assign various questions to various teams of new teachers and mentors. Working in teams, have each team unpack the question and prepare appropriate responses.

1. How do you change the content when you can't change the standards?

The standards remain constant—they determine what you teach in terms of concepts, skills, and attitudes—yet the actual content you use to deliver the information can change by complexity levels, the resources you use, and the actual learning environment.

2. How do you change the assignment and maintain the dignity of every student?

Teachers foster an awareness of differences in learners and of brain science facts about how every brain is different in how it accesses information. Learning preferences are designed into the curriculum and lessons, and differentiation becomes part of the classroom culture.

3. How do you assess various assignments for high school?

When different students do different assignments to accomplish the same goal, they are graded on how well they do their assignments; they are accessing the information differently. However, when it comes to grade point averages, the question takes on another dimension. Is an A for a simpler assignment equivalent to an A for a complex assignment? Obviously, the answer is "No." Although both students may meet the standard, the one who does the simple assignment is judged on a scoring rubric as meeting expectations, whereas the other with the more advanced assignment exceeds expectations. These concerns must be addressed in the calculation of grade point averages. Often a weighting of the assignments with allotted points is used to designate basic, average, or advanced assignments. District leaders and high school faculties must have this discussion and determine their policy for grading differentiated assignments.

4. How do teachers prepare all students for the test at their grade level?

In order to prepare all students for grade-level exams when they may be performing below the grade-level materials, explicit test preparation activities must occur. It is not fair to plunge students into testing situations without some familiarity with the types of tests, the types of questions, and the guidelines for acceptable responses. Sample questions, test-taking strategies, and attention to the tricks of testing well are appropriate preparation techniques. However, these test preparation strategies must be in balance with the teaching and learning processes of the class.

5. How do teachers do all this active, engaged learning and still keep up with the district or state pacing guide?

Active, engaged learning occurs in robust, integrated curriculum models such as problem-based and project-based learning and performance learning tasks. When various elements (concepts, skills, attitudes) are combined into a rich learning experience, the pace can remain brisk, yet the learning can strive for deep understanding. Pacing guides are signposts to keep teachers on track. They do not replace teacher creativity and ingenuity in designing rigorous, relevant, purposeful lessons.

6. How do teachers do cooperative learning in open concept, open space classrooms?

  A. You manage the noise level (6-inch voices) and movement (how to move a chair or desk).

  B. You create sound barriers whenever possible (curtains, bookcases, file cabinets).

  C. You find another area to use for the activity (gym, cafeteria, library, schoolyard).

7. How do teachers write a lesson for every child?

Teachers don't! Students who need that level of differentiation have individualized education programs written for them. What teachers do is modify and differentiate the basic lessons to fit the strengths and weaknesses of various students. They do not attempt to write an individual lesson for every child.

8. How do teachers differentiate for 120–150 students in high school?

Teachers have a robust repertoire of teaching strategies; they use multiple methods in teaching the lesson, and they often offer various kinds of tasks. It's like making a pot roast with potatoes and peas: Some use lots of salt and pepper, some omit the potatoes and use two servings of pot roast, others mix their peas with their potatoes. None of them gets an entirely different dinner; they just get the pot roast their way.

9. How do teachers coteach effectively?

They do basic plans and use a consistent color coding for various kinds of differentiating strategies. Then each can visit the lesson separately and make notes accordingly. They try to find time at lunch or before or after school to talk. They request time together in the schedule when it is possible to do so. They elicit principal support for these schedules.

10. What do teachers do to differentiate and address standards at the same time?

Teachers honor the standards for their content and their grade level, yet they change the delivery, process, and accessibility of the learning. They offer different doors for students to enter into the learning and different ways for them to show what they know.

11. How do teachers differentiate every single lesson?

Many teachers already differentiate their lessons. Teachers modify or shift their basic lessons easily for students. They differentiate in subtle yet effective ways. For those just starting, it eventually becomes a natural part of their planning.

12. How do teachers justify whole class direct instruction?

Teachers may introduce a lesson to the whole class and review the lesson as a direct instruction strategy. Yet they will also include learning centers in the elementary classrooms and learning stations within a block of instructional time in the middle and high school classroom. Whole group instruction is only one small part of the active, engaged classroom.

9

A Love Affair
With Assessment

Rubrics Are Our New Best Friend

The cynics say, "Assessment drives instruction," implying that all instructional decisions are governed by the assessment instruments that reign supreme in a district striving for excellence. When this culture thrives in a school, the teachers feel tremendous pressure to raise the students' test scores. Unfortunately, the well-intentioned dictate that strives for higher student achievement often leads teachers away from the robust teaching models and toward more didactic methods that stress skill-and-drill exercises resembling test-taking scenarios. In the end, teachers may become focused on teaching to the test rather than teaching for a lifetime.

> Assessment is instruction!
> Instruction is assessment!

Another way to think about assessment, and perhaps a more accurate observation of the process, is summed up in the saying, "Assessment is instruction! Instruction is assessment!" Assessment, when designed as authentic student performances, creates a need for what is called a backward design of curriculum and instruction. In this design process, based on the learning standards or educational goals, teachers decide what students need to know and be able to do. Once the goals are determined, teachers think about what evidence demonstrates that students know something and are able to do whatever they are expected to do. Then, in the final stage, teachers think about how they might appraise the quality of student learning. In the broadest sense, these assessments involve three distinct elements that are inextricably linked to instruction: the learning standard, the evidence of that learning, and the judgment about the quality of learning. With these interwoven elements clearly in mind, the teacher is able to design the learning in an informed and skillful way. Therefore, assessment does become instruction.

SHARE CRITERIA FOR SUCCESS WITH STUDENTS BEFORE THEY BEGIN THE TASK

The reverse is true also, because instruction that requires students to demonstrate what they know and what they are able to do is instruction that has the assessment built in. This is performance assessment in all its glory, and it is the essence of instructional methods that dictate performance tasks or authentic evidence and judgment (rubric) of the learning. The analogy might read like this:

Evidence : Judgment :: Performance task : Rubric

In this equation, assessment requires evidence of learning and, in turn, ways to judge that evidence in terms of the quality of that performance. This judgment of the performance task is best assessed through the use of a scoring guide or a rubric. In this way, the student performance is critiqued against criteria and indicators of how well the criteria are met. For example, a standard of learning may be as follows.

Standard: Goal

Students are able to demonstrate understanding and application of the principles of geometry.

Evidence: Performance Task

To design curricula and instruction that require students to show how well they understand and can apply one principle of geometry, the teacher might design a project learning unit. In this way, students can demonstrate their learning through the instructional experience, showing how the Pythagorean theorem and its 3, 4, 5 relationship helps to square a model structure. Working as partners or small cooperative groups, students are required to build two models. In one design the students construct a structure using the right triangle design based on the theorem and show that the structure is square. With the squareness comes quality. In a comparable design, they can demonstrate the lack of squareness when the "right triangle" structure is not used, and they can demonstrate the inferior quality of the structure. Thus, the performance task or the evidence is provided.

Judgment: Rubric

Now the teacher must judge the quality of the performance through the use of a scoring guide or rubric. This requires criteria and indicators of how well the criteria are met. Criteria for the project might include both content and process standards that would be recorded in the first column of Table 9.1. Indicators of the quality of the performance are shown in the top row.

Table 9.1   Indicators of Quality

Criteria	Developing	Competent	Proficient	Excellent
Completed models				
Illustrated theorem				
Accurate work				

In summary, to think of assessment as instruction and instruction as assessment, teachers use the backward design method for designing curriculum and instruction. In this way, teachers incorporate the standards of learning, the evidence of learning, and the judgment of the quality of the learning in complex tasks that engage students in the teaching and learning process. Thus, the assessment versus instruction conundrum is solved in one glorious project.

Film Clip: *Music of the Heart*

Focus: Performance Is the Ultimate Evidence of What Students Know and Are Able to Do

Find the clip in which the high standards of quality demanded by the teacher are clearly represented through the musical performance, demonstrating performance assessment, which is a natural outcome in the visual and performing arts.

Questions

What criteria are evident in high-quality musical performances, and how are they rated to quality indicators? Think about and discuss the many events in which skillful performances are judged (e.g., athletic tryouts, dance auditions, keyboarding tests, driver's education road tests, qualifying exams, artistic competitions).

Activity: ABC Graffiti Assessment

Using the alphabet as an advance organizer, have the new teachers, working in table teams, prepare a piece of chart paper with the ABCs. Demonstrate by showing the poster paper with two columns (Column 1, A–M and Column 2, N–Z). Have them place the word "assessment" at the top of the page.

Then, in a 3-minute blitz, have them brainstorm as many connections to the word "assessment" as they can. These are synonyms, phrases, or related words that come to mind. Anything goes because it is a brainstorm.

Have the teams rank the top three words that help unpack the concept of assessment and share the various responses from the table teams. Debrief. Delineate the myriad assessment techniques that are available to teachers and the rationale for using a diverse set of assessment tools.

10

A Winning Way With Parents

To Report, Relate, and Celebrate

S chooling is like a three-legged stool, supported by the student, the teacher, and the parent. Together they make the stool strong, sturdy, and structurally sound. Teachers and students benefit when parents are involved in the teaching and learning process. That involvement comes in a variety of forms: formal and informal reporting to parents, engagement of parents in volunteer work in the classroom or in the school, and invitations to parents to share in student performances and celebrations of student achievement.

> Schooling is like a three-legged stool, supported by the student, the teacher, and the parent. Together they make the stool strong, sturdy, and structurally sound.

WHAT IF PARENTS DO THESE 10 THINGS?

1. What if parents read to their child every day?

If parents read one book a day for the first 3 years, their child will have heard 1,000 stories by the age of 3.

> If parents read one book a day for the first 3 years, their child will have heard 1,000 stories by the age of 3.

2. What if parents teach their toddler all the nursery rhymes they know?

If parents teach their toddler all the nursery rhymes they know, they will empower their child with a sense of story.

3. What if parents create a print-rich environment of books, magazines, newspapers, and online reading?

If parents create a print-rich environment, their child will embrace a wealth of reading resources.

4. What if parents talk to their child in complete sentences, rich with new and needed words?

If parents talk to their child in rich, full sentences, their child will build a vast vocabulary.

5. What if parents ensure that their child has playtime on computers at every age?

If parents ensure that their child has playtime on a computer at every age, their child will be computer literate.

6. What if parents arrange a special time and place for homework?

If parents arrange a special time and place for homework, their child will learn the rewards of practice.

7. What if parents check the child's homework for accuracy and neatness?

If parents check the child's homework for accuracy and neatness, their child will exhibit precision and pride in his or her work.

8. What if parents volunteer at their child's school?

If parents volunteer at their child's school, their child will see teachers and parents as a team.

9. What if parents attend school functions and participate in robust ways?

If parents attend school functions and participate in robust ways, their child will learn to value school as an integral part of life.

10. What if parents communicate regularly with their child's teachers?

If parents communicate regularly with their child's teachers, the child will develop the means and the methods to communicate regularly.

Formal reporting to parents usually occurs through the use of report cards, parent conferences, meetings between school personnel and parents, and official phone calls to parents about students. When these formal communications occur, it is wise for teachers to remember to let the parents talk, too. Little real communication is happening if the teacher is doing all the talking. Teachers need to invite the parents to participate in the process and let them share their impressions first. Teachers might elicit responses from parents as the dialogue unfolds. Whenever possible and appropriate, teachers often invite the student to be a part of the conversation also. After all, it is in the student's best interest to take some ownership in the process.

INVOLVE PARENTS IN THE TEACHING AND LEARNING PROCESS

Informal ways of communicating and reporting to parents might include a class newsletter to parents describing past and future events, weekly or sometimes even daily notes on student papers and projects, memos to parents about special events, and individualized notes that communicate successes and concerns to keep the parent informed about students' lives at school. One teacher created two forms on half sheets of ditto paper, one called "Yea! Yea!" and the other called "Oops!" The "Yea! Yea!" form was sent home when students did something to cheer about: finished a book, got an A on a spelling test, helped someone who was hurt, shared lunch with a friend, or came up with a great question that day. The "Oops!" form was sent home when students did something of concern, something that did not seem too serious but warranted a note to the parents: pushing in the lunch line, not completing a daily assignment, disrupting another group, or demonstrating poor manners in the assembly.

Although the tenor of these frequent communications changes with the age groups of the students, the intent remains the same. The teacher must take the initiative to stay in touch with the parents. Through these notes, parents have frequent communication from the teacher that is both positive and negative. They open the lines of communication and keep them open if parents are required to sign the notes and return them to the teacher.

Teachers might create a class Web site to present information about the topics under study, upcoming events, instructions about how parents might help with homework, and student blogs or information about relevant educational issues. Depending on their age, the students might even create and maintain the Web site.

In addition to formal and informal communication with parents, there are opportunities to engage parents in volunteer work in the classroom. They make great reading partners in the young grades or willing helpers on field trips and other school excursions or projects. In one classroom, the teacher invited a team of parents to come in and assist students with a simple machine unit in which each student had to build a dragon with movable parts. The parent team helped the students who might not have a parent at home to help them. In the upper grades, parents can participate in similar ways with complex projects, field trips, or clerical duties or even as guest speakers in an area of expertise. The more the parents are linked to the classroom activities, the better their understanding of what the teaching and learning process is all about.

One final way of involving parents is by inviting them into the classroom for various performances, celebrations, or events culminating a unit of study. This strategy of getting parents to the school usually succeeds because every parent wants to see his or her student perform. And, of course, the students put some pressure on their parents to show up.

Everyone wins when the parents are involved in classroom events, school issues, and student activities.

Film Clip: *Mr. Holland's Opus*

Focus: Parents and Community

Show the porch scene in which Mr. Holland is challenged by his coach friend to teach a kid to "bang a drum." Follow the scene through the practice sessions to the performance of the marching band, when the drummer passes his proud parents.

Questions

How might teachers invite parents to participate in school? What can parents do to support the school success of their child? They can tap into the strategies of literacy and learning. Literacy matters! And learning is what school is all about. If kids can't, won't, or don't read, nothing else matters. Parents may not be reading teachers, but they know the power of being a literate person in our society.

They understand that the ability to read and write, to speak and listen, to use language to communicate, to read about history, scientific discoveries, and mathematical theories, to critique great literature and debate a telling point, to speak eloquently, to hear and be heard, and to write clearly are academic performances embraced by an educated person.

Activity: Cooperative Learning Tear and Share

Have new teachers work in groups of four. Have them count off by 1, 2, 3, and 4. Then ask them to fold a piece of paper into four corner sections and number the corners 1, 2, 3, and 4 as in Figure 10.1. Have them read the 10 parent suggestions listed earlier and answer all four questions on the form. After all participants have completed the responses, have them tear the paper into four sections and pass the appropriate numbered piece to the person with that number. Now, have each person summarize the four responses and in turn, give an oral summary of the answers. Debrief. Discuss how to get this kind of information to parents.

Figure 10.1   Cooperative Tear and Share: Parents

1. How does an ordinary nursery rhyme model good story text?	2. Prioritize the following three elements: ___ Space to do homework ___ Time to do homework ___ Checking the homework
3. Describe three tasks for parent volunteers.	4. Explain one method for parent communication that works for you.

Bibliography

Preface

Peter, L. I. (1977). *Peter's quotations: Ideas for our time.* New York: Morrow.

Pirsig, R. M. (1984). *Zen and the art of motorcycle maintenance.* New York: Bantam.

Strunk, W. J., & White, E. B. (2000). *The elements of style* (4th ed.). Needham Heights, MA: Allyn & Bacon.

Introduction

Pete, B., & Fogarty, R. (2005). *Close the achievement gap: Simple strategies that work.* Thousand Oaks, CA: Corwin Press.

#1. A Knowing Colleague

Ashton-Warner, S. (1986). *Teacher.* New York: Simon & Schuster.

Blanchard, K., & Johnson, S. (2000). *The one minute manager: Increase productivity, profits, and your own prosperity.* New York: HarperCollins.

Burke, K. (2002). *Mentoring guidebook level I: Starting the journey.* Thousand Oaks, CA: Corwin Press.

Codell, E. R. (1999). *Educating Esme: Diary of a teacher's first year.* Chapel Hill, NC: Algonquin Books.

Fogarty, R. (2001). *A model for mentoring our teacher: Centers of pedagogy.* Chicago: Fogarty & Associates.

Fogarty, R., & Pete, B. (2006). *From staff room to classroom: A guide for planning and coaching professional development.* Thousand Oaks, CA: Corwin Press.

Johnson, S. (1998). *Who moved my cheese?* New York: Putnam.

Schmuck, R., & Schmuck, P. (2000). *Group processes in the classroom.* Dubuque, IA: WCB/McGraw-Hill.

#2. A Place Called "My Room"

Bloom, B. (1981). *All our students learning.* New York: McGraw-Hill.

Caine, R. N., Caine, G., McClintic, C., & Klimek, K. (2004). *12 brain/mind learning principles in action: The fieldbook for making connections, teaching, and the human brain.* Thousand Oaks, CA: Corwin Press.

Costa, A. L. (1991). *The school as a home for the mind: A collection of articles.* Thousand Oaks, CA: Corwin Press.

Costa, A., & Kallick, B. (2000). *Habits of mind.* Alexandria, VA: Association for Supervision and Curriculum Development.

Csikszentmihalyi, M. (1990). *Flow: The psychology of optimal experience.* New York: Harper & Row.

Diamond, M., & Hopson, J. (1999). *Magic trees of the mind.* New York: Penguin.

Goleman, D. (1997). *Emotional intelligence.* New York: Bantam.

Goodlad, J. I. (1994). *A place called school.* New York: McGraw-Hill.

Lewkowicz, A. B. (2006). *Teaching emotional intelligence: Strategies and activities for helping students make effective choices* (2nd ed.). Thousand Oaks, CA: Corwin Press.

Marcus, S. (2007). *The hungry brain: The nutrition/cognition connection.* Thousand Oaks, CA: Corwin Press.

#3. A Method for Managing

Block, J., & Anderson, L. W. (1975). *Mastery learning in classroom instruction.* New York: Macmillan.

Bosch, K. (2006). *Planning classroom management: A five-step process to creating a positive learning environment* (2nd ed.). Thousand Oaks, CA: Corwin Press.

Guskey, T. R. (Ed.). (1994). *High-stakes performance assessment: Perspectives on Kentucky's educational reform.* Thousand Oaks, CA: Corwin Press.

Hunter, M. (1971). *Teach for transfer.* El Segundo, CA: TIP Publications.

Joyce, B., & Weil, M. (2000). *Models of teaching* (6th ed.). Needham Heights, MA: Allyn & Bacon.

Marzano, R. (2003). *Classroom management.* Alexandria, VA: Association for Supervision and Curriculum Development.

#4. A Discipline Plan

Burke, K. (2000). *What to do with the kid who . . . : Developing cooperation, self-discipline, and responsibility in the classroom* (2nd ed.). Thousand Oaks, CA: Corwin Press.

Evertson, C., Emmer, E. T., Clements, B. S., & Worsham, M. E. (1997). *Classroom management for elementary teachers.* Boston: Allyn & Bacon.

Jones, V. F., & Jones, L. S. (1998). *Comprehensive classroom management: Creating communities of support and solving problems* (5th ed.). Boston: Allyn & Bacon.

Marzano, R. (2003). *Classroom management.* Alexandria, VA: Association for Supervision and Curriculum Development.

Wolfgang, C. H. (1999). *Solving discipline problems: Methods and models for today's teachers* (4th ed.). Boston: Allyn & Bacon.

#5. An Understanding of Standards

Burke, K. (2005). *How to assess authentic learning* (4th ed.). Thousand Oaks, CA: Corwin Press.

Fogarty, R. (2001). *Standards of learning: A blessing in disguise.* Chicago: Fogarty & Associates.

Marzano, R., & Kendall, J. S. (1996). *A comprehensive guide to designing standards-based districts, schools, and classrooms.* Alexandria, VA: Association for Supervision and Curriculum Development and Mid-Continent Regions Educational Laboratory.

Perna, D. M., & Davis, J. R. (2006). *Aligning standards and curriculum for classroom success* (2nd ed.). Thousand Oaks, CA: Corwin Press.

Wiggins, G., & McTighe, J. (1998). *Understanding by design.* Alexandria, VA: Association for Supervision and Curriculum Development.

#6. A Known Knowledge Base

Beane, J. (Ed.). (1995). *Toward a coherent curriculum: 1995 yearbook of the ASCD.* Alexandria, VA: Association for Supervision and Curriculum Development.

Burke, K. (2006). *From standards to rubrics in six steps: Tools for assessing student learning, K–8.* Thousand Oaks, CA: Corwin Press.

Costa, A., & Kallick, B. (2000). *Habits of mind: A developmental series.* Alexandria, VA: Association for Supervision and Curriculum Development.

Fogarty, R. (2002). *How to integrate the curricula* (2nd ed.). Thousand Oaks, CA: Corwin Press.

Jacobs, H. (1990). *Interdisciplinary curriculum: Design and implementation.* Alexandria, VA: Association for Supervision and Curriculum Development.

#7. A Fail-Safe Lesson Design

Fogarty, R. (1994). *How to teach metacognitive reflection.* Thousand Oaks, CA: Corwin Press.

Fogarty, R. (2001). *Brain-compatible classrooms* (2nd ed.). Thousand Oaks, CA: Corwin Press.

Fogarty, R. (2001). *Standards of learning: A blessing in disguise.* Chicago: Fogarty & Associates.

Fogarty, R. (in press). Architects of the intellect. In A. Costa (Ed.), *Developing minds: A resource book for teaching thinking* (2nd ed.). Alexandria, VA: Association for Supervision and Curriculum Development.

Johnson, D., Johnson, R., & Holubec, E. J. (1986). *Circles of learning: Cooperation in the classroom.* Alexandria, VA: Association for Supervision and Curriculum Development.

Kagan, S. (1992). *Cooperative learning structures.* San Clemente, CA: Kagan Cooperative.

Perkins, D. (1992). *Smart schools: From training memories to educating minds.* New York: Free Press.

Perkins, D. (1995). *Outsmarting IQ: The emerging science of learnable intelligence.* New York: Free Press.

Skowron, J. (2006). *Powerful lesson planning: Every teacher's guide to effective instruction* (2nd ed.). Thousand Oaks, CA: Corwin Press.

Slavin, R. (1983). *Cooperative learning.* New York: Longman.

#8. A Repertoire of Teaching Strategies

Berman, S. (2006). *Service learning: A guide to planning, implementing, and assessing student projects* (2nd ed.). Thousand Oaks, CA: Corwin Press.

Fogarty, R. (1997). *Problem-based learning & other curriculum models for the multiple intelligences classroom.* Thousand Oaks, CA: Corwin Press.

Fogarty, R. (2001). *Making sense of the research on the brain and learning.* Chicago: Fogarty & Associates.

Fogarty, R. (2006). *Literacy matters: Strategies every teacher can use* (2nd ed.). Thousand Oaks, CA: Corwin Press.

Fogarty, R., & Pete, B. (2005). *How to differentiate curriculum, instruction and assessment.* Thousand Oaks, CA: Corwin Press.

Gardner, H. (1983). *Frames of mind: The theory of multiple intelligences.* New York: Basic Books.

Gardner, H. (1993). *Multiple intelligences: The theory in practice.* New York: HarperCollins.

Haycock, K. *Teachers matter . . . a lot* [newsletter]. Washington, DC: Education Trust.

Joyce, B., & Weil, M. (2000). *Models of teaching* (6th ed.). Needham Heights, MA: Allyn & Bacon.

Keene, E. O., & Zimmerman, S. (1997). *Mosaic of thought.* Portsmouth, NH: Heinemann.

Kovalic, S. (1993). *ITI: The model: Integrated thematic instruction.* Village of Oak Creek, AZ: Books for Educators.

Marzano, R., Pickering, D., & Pollock, J. (2001). *Classroom instruction that works.* Alexandria, VA: Association for Supervision and Curriculum Development.

Pete, B., & Fogarty, R. (2003). *Nine best practices that make the difference.* Thousand Oaks, CA: Corwin Press.

Pete, B., & Fogarty, R. (2005). *Close the achievement gap: Simple strategies that work.* Thousand Oaks, CA: Corwin Press.

Tomlinson, C. A. (1999). *The differentiated classroom: Responding to the needs of all learners.* Alexandria, VA: Association for Supervision and Curriculum Development.

#9. A Love Affair With Assessment

Burke, K. (2004). *Performance assessment: Evidence of learning.* Chicago: Fogarty & Associates.

Burke, K. (2005). *How to assess authentic learning* (4th ed.). Thousand Oaks, CA: Corwin Press.

Burke, K., Fogarty, R., & Belgrad, S. (2002). *The portfolio connection: Student work linked to standards* (2nd ed.). Thousand Oaks, CA: Corwin Press.

Fogarty, R. (1999). *Balanced assessment.* Thousand Oaks, CA: Corwin Press.

Fogarty, R. (1999). *How to raise test scores.* Thousand Oaks, CA: Corwin Press.

O'Connor, K. (2002). *How to grade for learning: Linking grades to standards* (2nd ed.). Thousand Oaks, CA: Corwin Press.

Popham, W. J. (1999). *Classroom assessment: What teachers need to know* (2nd ed.). Boston: Allyn & Bacon.

Stiggins, R. (1994). *Student-centered classroom assessment.* New York: Macmillan.

#10. A Winning Way With Parents

Burke, K. (2005). *How to assess authentic learning* (4th ed.). Thousand Oaks, CA: Corwin Press.

Burke, K., Fogarty, R., & Belgrad, S. (2002). *The portfolio connection: Student work linked to standards* (2nd ed.). Thousand Oaks, CA: Corwin Press.

Fox, M. (2001). *Reading magic.* San Diego, CA: Harcourt.

Schiller, D. P., & Caroll, M. K. (1986). *A research-based approach to improving instruction.* Oxford, OH: National Staff Development Council.

Walberg, H. L. (1984). Families as partners in educational productivity. *Phi Delta Kappan, 65*(6), 397–400.

Index

**CORWIN
PRESS**

The Corwin Press logo—a raven striding across an open book—represents the union of courage and learning. Corwin Press is committed to improving education for all learners by publishing books and other professional development resources for those serving the field of PreK–12 education. By providing practical, hands-on materials, Corwin Press continues to carry out the promise of its motto: **"Helping Educators Do Their Work Better."**